1

To my parents,

Hi

Welcome all to this EBook on how to start your Home Based Online Business which will help you earn 7 figures every year.

My name is Abhimanyu Datta and I will teach you how you can start your own business in low investment using Internet.

Let me tell you how I started my business. It was 2010 right after my MBA that I left my city Mumbai and moved to Delhi for job. I worked in a company that sold internet ads. At that time internet advertising had begun to take importance in the business world. Unfortunately I had to leave that job because I had a medical emergency.

So I did job in another company and a failed attempt in applying to defense forces where I failed to cleared the interview, I decided to join my family business. I joined in

the June 2011 and started working very hard in my family business.

As days and months passed by I realized two things:

1. My business has no guarantee and the profits are reducing day by day

2. I need another source of income, preferably a business which I can call mine. Where how I do business is in my

control and also how much I earn.

With these 2 things in mind my quest for searching the business that will suit me started. I thought to myself what I can do that can help me in earning money easily. Because I knew that I am not a person who can do cold calls, visit offices and talk to strangers.

I was ready to learn about Marketing & Business. But I was very clear about one thing.

I wanted to create a system using the modern digital tools that can automate my business and bulk of the things is managed by the apps.

Then one day I stumbled upon a YouTube video of Vivek Bindra. So now you would ask what was so special in it. I realized a very simple thing.

It was that Vivek Bindra was teaching in his video about business and in the comments a lot of people had asked him to call them to guide them to solve their problem. Basically people approached Vivek Bindra and asked him to provide his services to them.

This was a light bulb moment for me. I understood 3 things from it:

1. Anyone can teach a subject for which they are passionate about.

2. When you teach, you create an authority for yourself in the eyes of the people. Hence

people start contacting you for your services. Basically people start running behind you and chasing you. Isn't it fantastic? It's a dream come true for any entrepreneur / business owner.

3. When I read T. Harv Eker (renowned business coach & guru) blog where he said teaching is the best way to get rich. This statement made sense to me when I saw Vivek Bindra video.

So I understood that if you have to start your own business then teaching people is the best way to earn money and build a stable business for you. And the best way is to build an online business which can be done from anywhere and anytime with my laptop, mobile phone & internet connection. I will tell you in some time the whole plan about it, and how you can also start for yourself.

Now stay with me for a second. I know when you hear the word teach you might be thinking that is it teaching the school or college courses to students. No it's not!

Well we teach people about various subjects that people want to learn related to life and business. Now you might be thinking how teaching will work in the business.

Because when we hear the word business, we imagine selling some product, service or some subscription service or plan right?

Because when you google the definition of business it comes up with this:

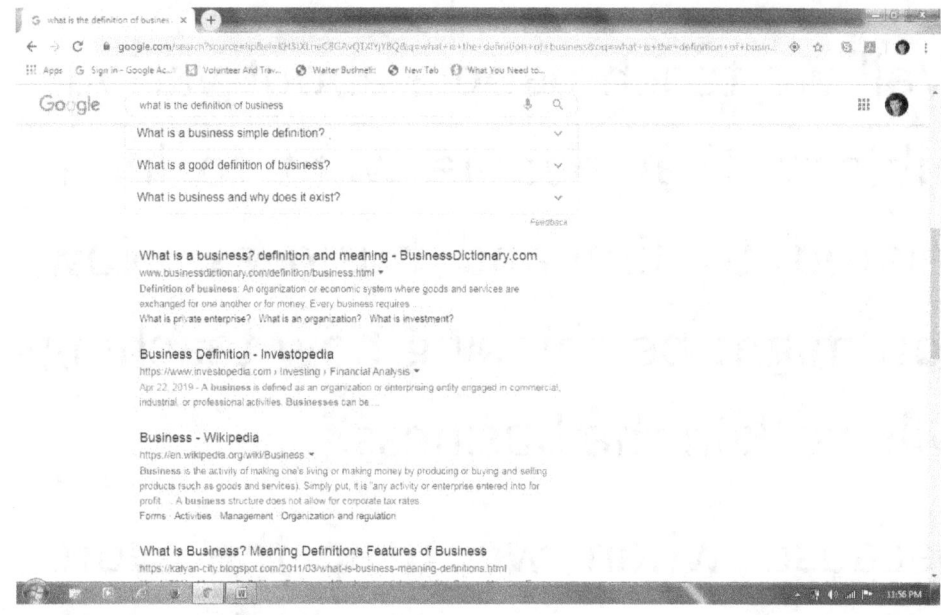

See look at the first results in google. All of them say selling of product or service for the exchange of money or with a goal to earn profit.

But what we are doing here is that we don't tell why they should buy our product, service or plan. What we are doing here is when we are teaching; we are creating authority about our subject, respect and trust in the mind of the people.

Hence we purchase things from people whom we trust, and who has authority in their field.

Now if you agree with what I have said, you can keep continue to read ahead.

Now you will have 2 thoughts going in your mind:

1. How will I come with so much content for videos/blogs? I don't have the team & the equipment to make such videos. I don't know how to write for a blog

2. Which niche category should I choose? Will it be profitable? How do I choose the niche that I am expert in?

What is niche category?

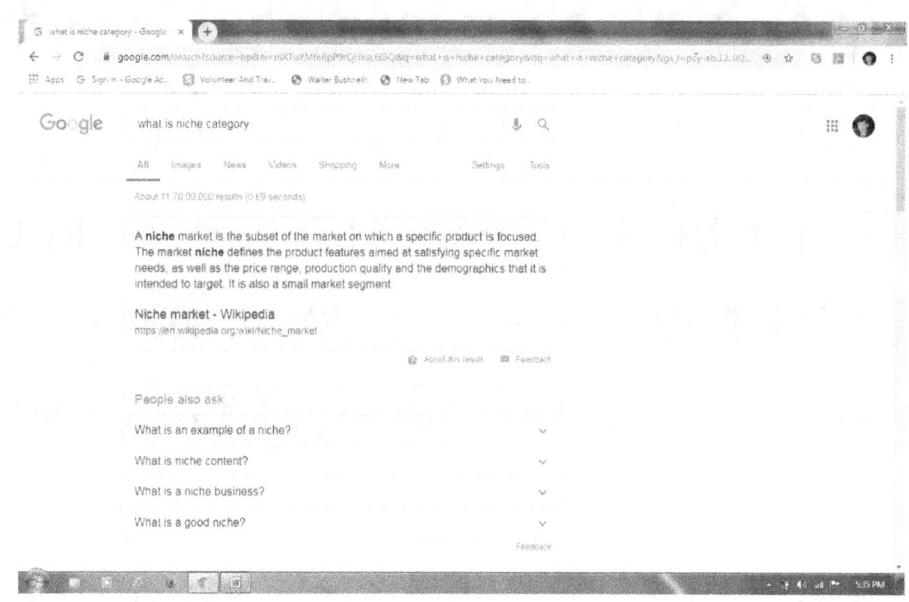

In simple words it is a subset of an existing market segment.

That is where the real and huge money is.

I know many of you who are reading this eBook will be having the question in their mind that how do I know what you are feeling?

Don't be surprised that how I know it? I have been in your place so I know it's pretty natural to have such questions. And if you stay with me a little longer I will answer your these questions as well.

So now we will look at the steps that you have wanted to know for such a long time.

1. Deciding the Niche Category

So the first step in setting up your online home based business is to decide the product / service / idea / franchise niche for yourself.

I can't stress how important it is in your goal of setting up your online home based business. Because all the teaching and information that will revolve around the chosen niche product / service / franchise. It will form the crux or the base of your business plan.

It's really important that you do this step very carefully and choose the one that suits your personality & also has good market demand.

A good way to select it is to focus on evergreen areas in the business.

For example: Businesses related to food, healthcare, finance, business training, and any revolutionary idea.

For example, when internet came no one how big it would become. No one thought that Digital Marketing would be taught to people one day and whole line of new business would be born out of it. And see today people have become millionaires through business of digital marketing.

- So what you really need is vision about the business, passion about the subject and a good system to monetize it.

- Take your time and decide what will suit your personality.
- Check whether the company you are associating with has a good reputation and is in business for a long time

- Check whether the company which is offering you the product / service / franchise has inbuilt system that automates most of the business processes.

- Is the company present in multiple countries or limited countries? As an online business owner you would like to do business in as many as countries as possible

- The product should have repeat demand and should be a consumable product. This is very important for any individual who is trying to set their own home based business. Because you would like that once the information has been given, then the business should keep happening on auto pilot mode.

- That means that even if you are sleeping the business is happening. The customers are purchasing the goods from the online system. And your account is being credited with your profit. This is happening because you have taught them how their life would become easier and how the most pressing problem in their life would solve.

Best part of teaching business is there is no pressure or convincing from your side. It will just have an offer to connect with you for more info if they are interested. This is where the business happens and money exchanges hand. That is what we want. That people approach you and ask you about your product or service that you are offering.

You are comfortable when someone approaches you with a problem to solve or to help them with something.

2.   <u>Sign Up</u>

Once you have zeroed in on the product / service / franchise niche and you have researched the company then next step is to Sign Up with that company.

Now you would think that isn't it supposed to be my business. Why should I sign up from some company? I could very well sell my stuff under my own brand? Well then think about it. In this big world everything is run by brands. Let's for example say which phone brand are you using? It would be Apple, Samsung, Motorola or some other famous brand.

Even when we purchase anything related to finance like travel insurance or investment product what's the first thing we look at? What's the name of the company? How many branches it has got? And so on. No one feels comfortable to buy from an unknown brand.

So like way when you are starting your business it is always better to sign up with some reputed company. The benefit is that when you have developed your authority & trust and when people would approach you for advice, it would be easier for you to close the sale.

Once you have taught them, they would know that how your product or service can help them with. And when you recommend them something that has a brand name, and then the chance of the person buying from you increases by 93%.

Most of these companies have a very simple sign up process. And it does not require any upfront investment, registration charges or any other kind of charges.

3.   Learn about the business

There's a famous quote by Richard Branson owner of Virgin Business.

"If somebody offers you an amazing opportunity but you are not sure you can do it say yes then learn how to do it later!

This is exactly what I am saying here. You looked at the opportunity and you sign up.

Now you will learn how to do it. For this I would recommend that you hire a coach or a mentor to help with you it. Ask someone who has been already been doing the same business that you are planning to start.

Hiring a coach / mentor has many benefits:

- You would know the exact steps that you will take from Day 1

- Which means you will start earning money from day 1. You won't feel lost as you will have the support of the coach /mentor on a continuous basis.

\- You won't take it easy unless you have reached a certain level in your business and the coach / mentor will make sure that you stick to your goal.

Don't see hiring a mentor / coach as an expense but as an investment. There are many times when you approach someone from the same business that they will be happy to assist you and coach you in your business.

So make sure that when you learn about how to do your business you learn in an organized manner. And a coach / mentor are the best way to learn about it. This investment will pay you 100, 1000 even 10000 times your investment in the future.

4. <u>Decide your goal & plan for it</u>

Before starting any activity or doing anything in your life we always think about WHY? Why we are doing a particular thing.

What outcomes do we want? What are our goals? What do we want from that activity?

Same way when starting your home based online business it's important to understand why you are doing the business. What goals you want to achieve when you earn money from the business.

It's not always about the money for everyone. Sometimes it's about the future security that you want to build for your family. For someone it might be a way to fulfill their goals of travelling. For some it might be a way to get out of the job debt cycle. For some it might be a way to clear old debts. For some it may be a way to fulfill their some other goals like living away from city, travel the world, building another source of income for your family.

It can be anything. Whatever that is please write it down. Because your WHY will drive you to keep working in your home based online business consistently.

Remember this, a business without a goal is not a business, it's a dream. And dream never gets fulfilled unless you have a plan.

So write down your goal. Make your plan. Take the help of your coach / mentor from whom you learnt about the business.

But don't go without planning and preparation. Or you will lose badly.

There is a saying in Army that teaches its soldiers in their training.

The more your train and practice the less you bleed in the war.

So have a goal, have a detailed plan and then put it to action.

5. <u>Digital Tools for Your Business:</u>

Now comes the part where everything connects and will make sense to you. So there are lots of tools on the internet that you can use to build your business. There are paid as well as free tools. But we are going to talk about free tools only.

So the first free tool is Google My Business. This is a very powerful tool that has been made available to everyone for free. The best part about this is that it is also for those people who provide services like yoga teachers, dance teachers, instructors, coaches etc.

It also will give you a simple format website where you describe about your business. You can also pictures about your business, videos of client testimonials.

It works on google searches and maps. Like for example when you search for car mechanics in say Bandra West it will shows you the names, addresses, pictures and also locations of the mechanics on the maps closest to your present location.

This is one of the best and cheapest ways to generate leads for your business if you understand how your customer will search for you on the search engine. Then using those keywords you can list your business on Google.

This topic alone will take another training EBook, but if you learn how to use it effectively to generate leads, then it's the most potent tool that will generate lots of profits for you.

2nd tool is ZOOM Application for virtual meetings. The most difficult part for any entrepreneur is that it takes a lot of time travelling in any city to meet people. With zoom you can do more meetings in the time you spend travelling.

Best part about zoom is that your personal information is safe and the other person won't be able to call you back on video mode. Best part this tool is also free.

With this tool you can also show presentations, spreadsheets as it gives you the option of sharing your screen with other participants on the call. So you can have 121 meetings or 1 to many meetings / group meetings as well at the same time.

So if you are planning to do a free seminar then it's a very good tool along with Facebook group where you can use FB live feature.

Optimizing your presence on social media is relatively easy. If you are willing to learn about it you can master it in a few weeks.

Now all these techniques require patience.

Business empires are not built in a day or a month or even a year.

Also combining multiple media platforms will give you a robust pipeline of continuous prospect leads; build your influence, authority and trust.

Now the next question in your mind would be how would I make such intriguing content. I am not an expert in it. Or I am not comfortable being in front of the camera.

Most of us feel uncomfortable at the idea of standing in front of the camera, or making valuable content every day.

Well, don't worry. Because I teach people how to do it.

How to create YouTube videos without facing the camera?

How to make valuable content every day?

How to never run out of content?

About the niche category I can help you in 2 ways:

First is if you have decided that in which category your business will exist or you have an existing business but you need my help in creating a niche around it, then I will help you in it.

I will brainstorm with you personally. I will help you create a complete strategy with complete plan around it so that you can confidently launch it.

Second, if you really liked it and understood of how you can start your online home based business but you are not sure of the niche you want to select then you have the option of joining with me in the niche I am already working in.

This niche has all the systems in place. It will be simple plug and play for you. The only thing I will need form you is that you should have patience, open mind, willingness to learn something new and enthusiasm for your new business.

You will be a part of my exciting team. Team SUKHOI

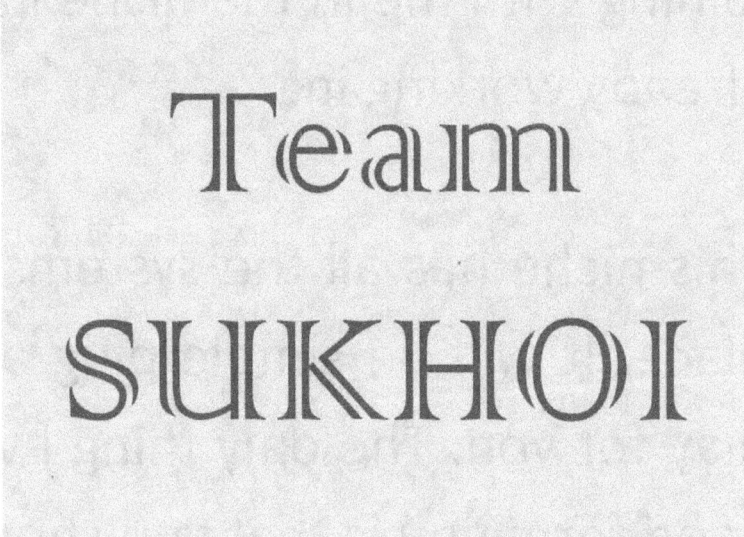

When you join me you will get personal mentoring and

coaching from me. I will handhold you personally in your new business in the initial 15 – 20 days to build your confidence.

I have built this exciting culture in my team. Where we even pat on the back for the activities you undertake even though if it does not generate results.

We recognize people for their effort, result and we reward you for the small goals that you achieve. Because we even celebrate small wins.

You might have a goal of earning few extra thousands or a hundred thousand (lakhs) in a month.

We have set process & system, where you plug in your goals and put in your efforts, you will get the result.

I expect few things from you when you join my team.

I respect professionalism.

I look for people with self-drive, enthusiasm, resilience, being responsible towards their business and undying positive spirit even in the most trying circumstances.

If you are still excited to join my team,

Call me @ +91 – 99673 84092
(9 AM – 8 PM) on weekdays and
11 AM to 4 PM on weekends

If my number is not reachable you can mail @ datta.abhimanyu@gmail.com

Use the subject line "Home based online business – Ref your EBook"

Connect with me on Facebook @ www.facebook.com/dattaabhimanyu

www.ingramcontent.com/pod-product-compliance
Lightning Source LLC
Chambersburg PA
CBHW080846170526
45158CB00009B/2650